The Curious Tale of the Dodo

The Dodo

Raphus Cucullatus

Have you heard the story about the Dodo bird? A bird I can only describe as "quite absurd!"

A story of a bird that could not fly or swim. Have you ever heard of such a strange thing?

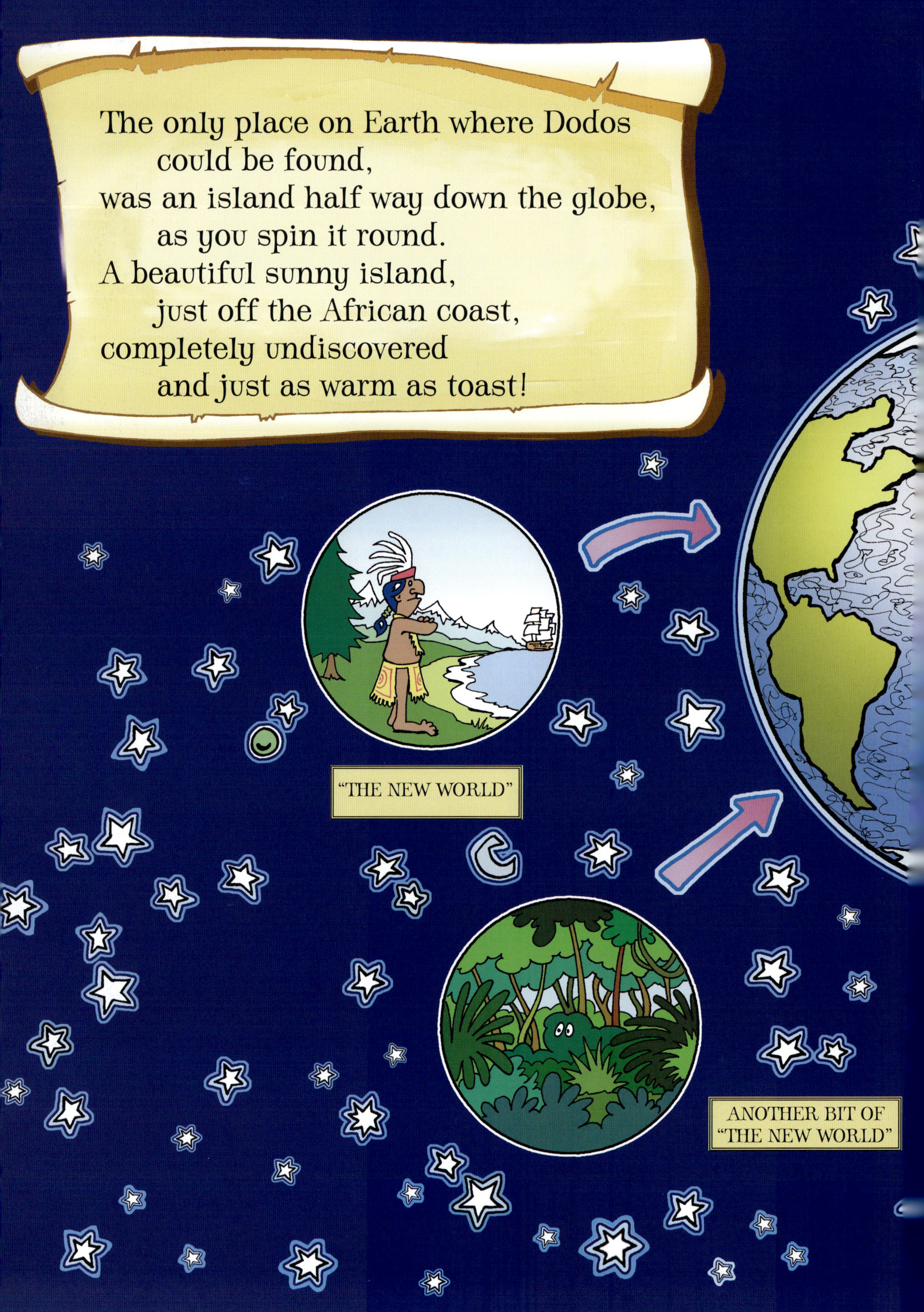
The only place on Earth where Dodos
could be found,
was an island half way down the globe,
as you spin it round.
A beautiful sunny island,
just off the African coast,
completely undiscovered
and just as warm as toast!
"THE NEW WORLD"
ANOTHER BIT OF
"THE NEW WORLD"

NORTH
POLE
DODO
ISLAND
SOUTH
POLE

This far away island is known as Mauritius.
Home to the Dodo, extinct but not fictitious.
A long, long time ago,
in fact over three hundred years,
Is when this story starts -
though it sadly ends in tears.

It is now known that Dodos
could not even swim!
A bird needs webbed feet
for that sort of thing!
But stranger still, as hard as they might try,
they had the wrong kind of wings
with which to fly!

It was on the far horizon
	that a tall ship appeared.
And by the time it anchored the Dodos thought
	"Hmmm, humans - weird!"
But being such friendly creatures
	and always so polite
They greeted the landing sailors
	with innocent delight.

Old Tub

Old Tub

The Dodos and sailors
lived happily together,
But sadly that feeling
did not last forever.
Short of food,
with no shops or fridge freezers,
those men became desperate
and hungry geezers!

Even the old Captain
was getting decidedly thinner,
and so would YOU
on just dry biscuits for dinner!
He screamed, “I must, I must eat something proper.”
So cook hurried ashore, carrying his large chopper!

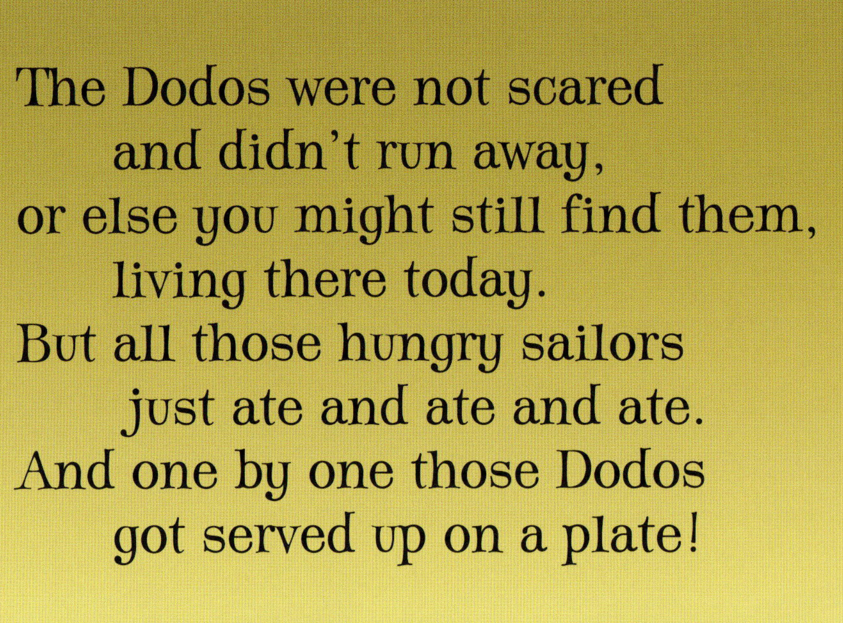

The Dodos were not scared
and didn't run away,
or else you might still find them,
living there today.
But all those hungry sailors
just ate and ate and ate.
And one by one those Dodos
got served up on a plate!

As time went by
    the Dodos were not so easily found.
Where had they all gone?
    Had they gone to ground?
The captain told his sailors,
    "Search the island high and low!"
But they'd eaten their last Dodo
    and didn't even know!!

Menu
Dodo
Dodo
Dodo
Dodo
or Dodo

Oh those greedy sailors!
What a terrible thing to have done.
Taking more then they really needed,
by killing every one!
But the sailors did not feel guilty.
They had no sense of shame.
Those Dodos had been an easy meal,
almost a kind of game.

The ship left Mauritius
Dodoless and very, very bare!
A species gone, a poorer world,
wasn't that unfair?
So was this the end of the Dodos?
Was this their final fate?
Could the sailors have been stopped
before it was too late?

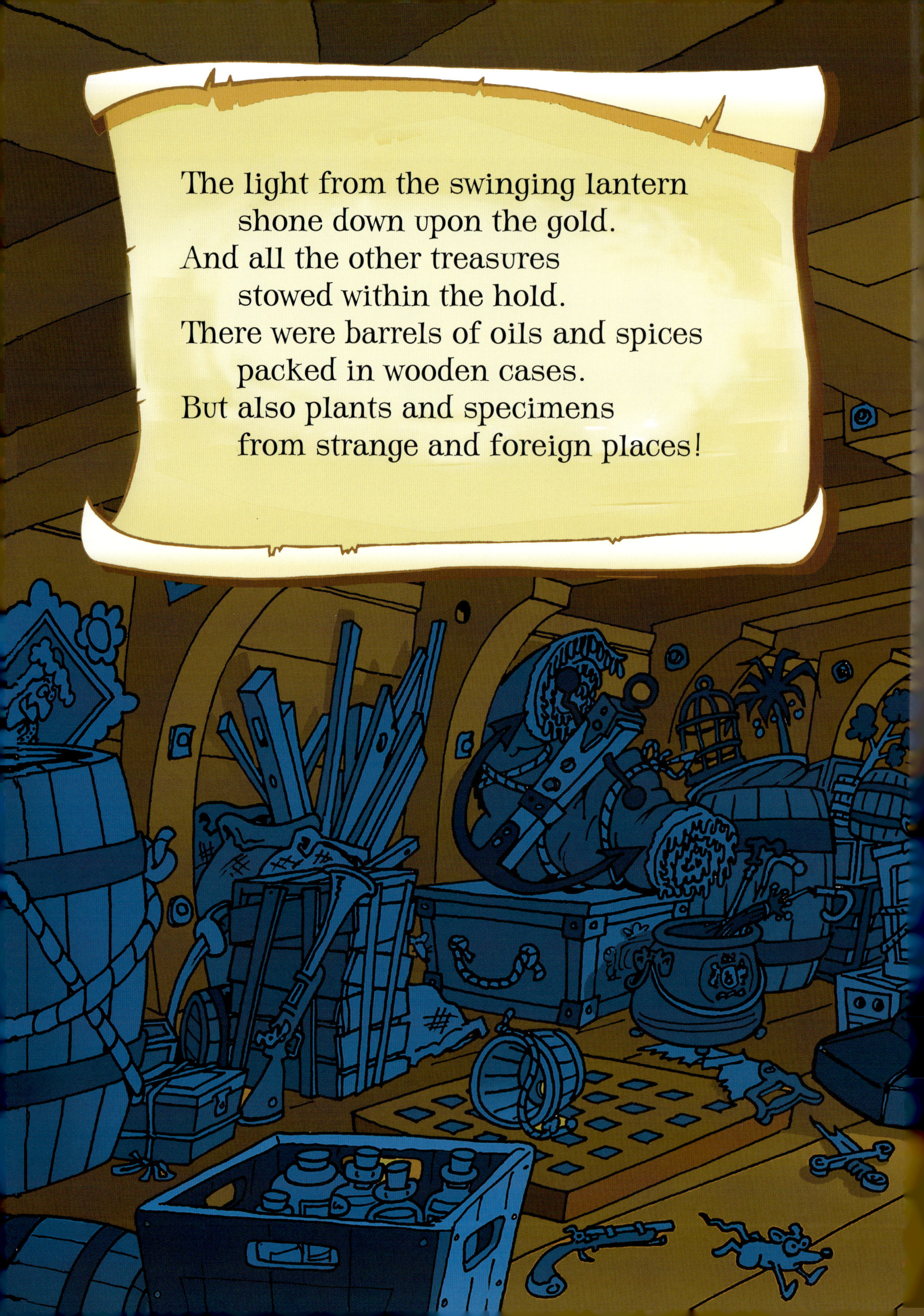
The light from the swinging lantern
shone down upon the gold.
And all the other treasures
stowed within the hold.
There were barrels of oils and spices
packed in wooden cases.
But also plants and specimens
from strange and foreign places!

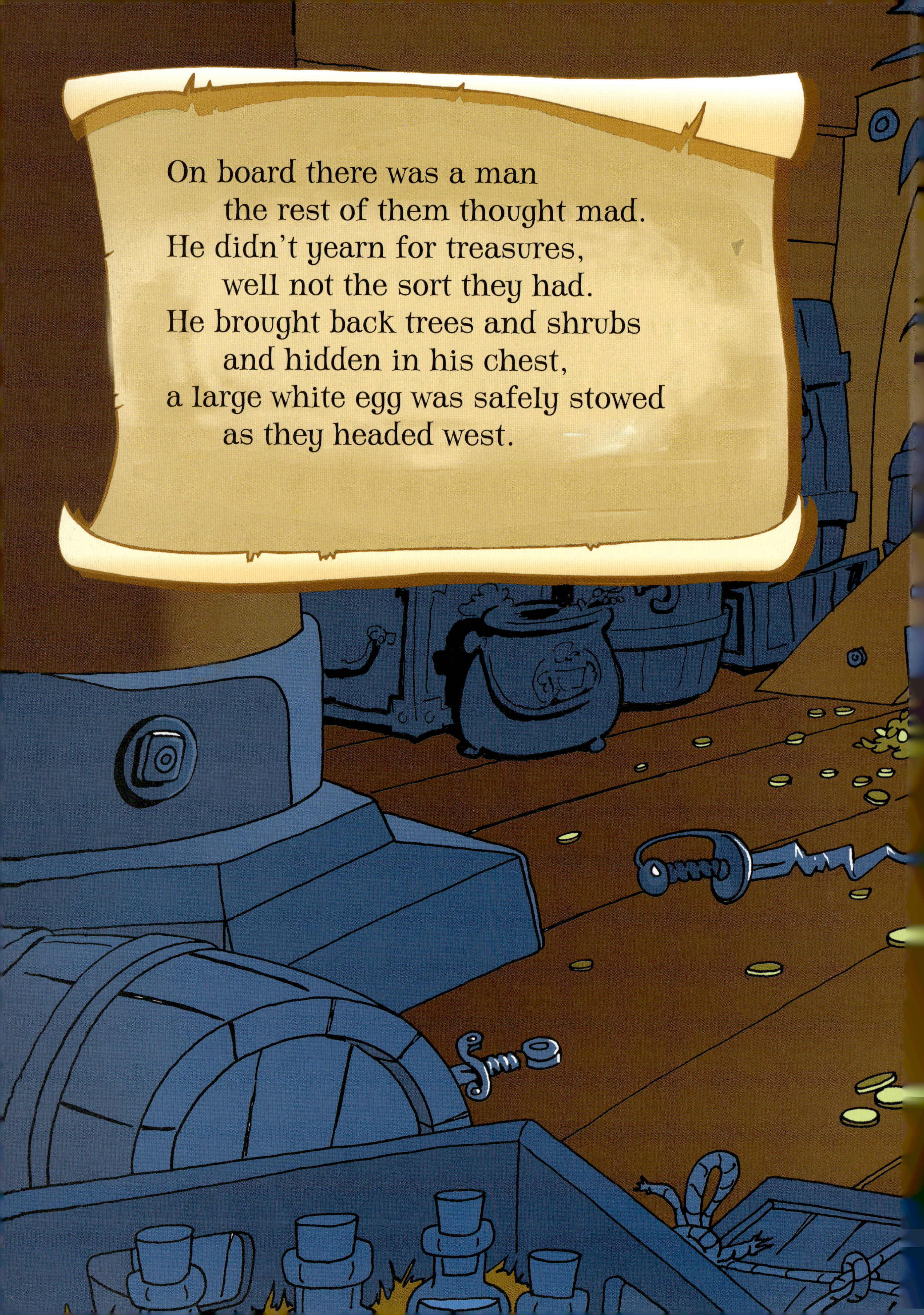

On board there was a man
the rest of them thought mad.
He didn't yearn for treasures,
well not the sort they had.
He brought back trees and shrubs
and hidden in his chest,
a large white egg was safely stowed
as they headed west.

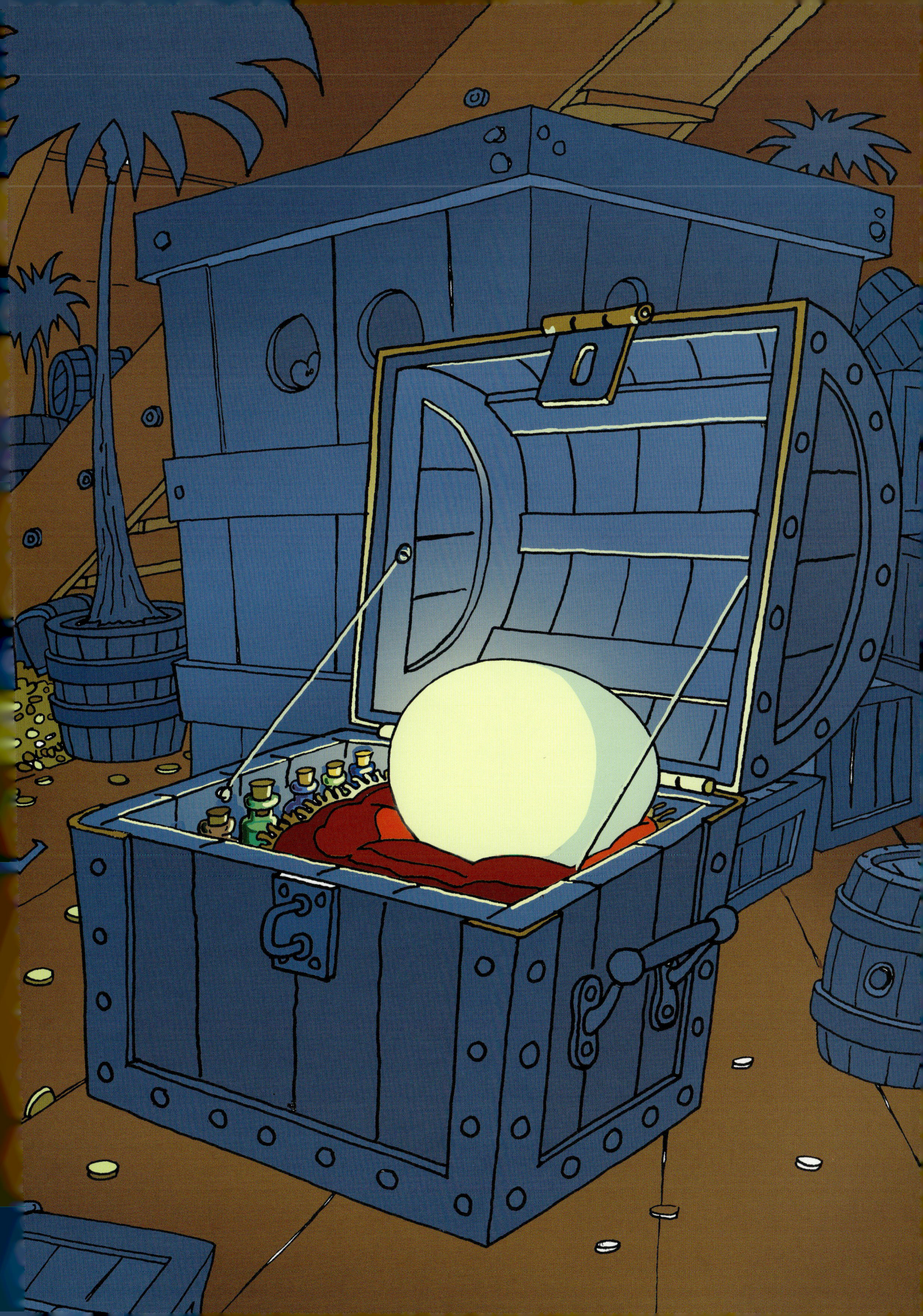

The ship sailed to Europe and
then to the New World,
where the tale and its mystery,
would one day be unfurled.
What became of the
chest?
What became of
the egg ?
Is the Dodo still
alive?
. . . Or am I
pulling
your
leg?